POEMS AND PROSE

PHILLIP MAGAÑA

Adela!
Thanks for your friendship
and for being you! Always
keep your head up!

Philly Magaña
7·26·'18

Poems and Prose

By Phillip Magaña

Published by Phillip Magaña at CreateSpace

CreateSpace Edition, License Notes

Book 2.

Took me forever to publish another one, but I'm doing it.

SINGLE DAD was the first to drop. A collection of posts from Facebook and Tumblr made into an ebook you can find on Smashwords.

I didn't think a book of poetry would be my second drop. After I made an Instagram account to promote a very failed attempt at doing an online biz, I started seeing and reading all the IG poetry folks were going crazy over.

Each writer with their own flavor, style, and viewpoint. I read it all, even if there was a common thread (to me, it was male bashing while the woman did no wrong), but I loved reading it. One day, I decided to give it a shot, and I haven't looked back.

I wrote poems from an obvious male perspective, and also from a "street" view. My stuff's about things I would tell myself looking from the inside out, not the other way. These are poems as if Phillip Of Days of Future Past and Present were at a BBQ, talking shit and drinking whiskey, telling stories about our life together, and hopefully, to drop some knowledge on someone who might need it.

Not only that, my writings were therapeutic for me. It helped me explore thoughts and feelings I didn't want to deal with, but it happened, and it helped. And yes, I got plenty more coming, but one book at a time.

I hope you'll walk my journey with me. Who knows, one day I'll be able to read your journey.

Peace.

PM
4/2/18

The Juice

VOLUME 1

"Bare As"

Bare room,
a lot like my soul.
Damn shame I feel the same way
when you're sitting next to me.

What's gonna change that,
is us going our separate ways.
That way,
the wall will disappear,
and the hate flung around the room
will cease.

10/24/17

Storytime: *LOVE BY THE MOON*

He asks:"What day is it?"

She replies: "You're turning day."

She reaches up on tiptoes to kiss this beast of a man she's fallen for. Now they'll always be together.

Alpha and Beta, as it should be. They strip naked, baring all. She jumps on him, wrapping arms and legs around him on this cool fall night, half moon above, hearts beating rapidly between them.

"Now and forever", he says, looking into her yellow eyes.

"I wouldn't have it any other way."

She tilts his head to the side, her fangs extrude. She bites deep but he doesn't flinch. This is what he wants. Her love, her pack, her everything.

He feels her "magic" enter him and it burns like hell. He buckles to his knees, still holding on to his Alpha.

She hangs on as she releases his neck, lying his limp head down slowly and cradling it in her lap.

"See the new you in a day, boo. You'll love this new

life." She kisses his forehead and looks at the moon. She won't be alone anymore, and neither will he. Live by the light, love by the moon. That's her people's way.

The werewolf way.

10/25/17

"Walk Alone"

No one likes being alone.
Solitude used to be a representation
of a person's strength.

A bond between person, soul, and
nature.
It used to be a badge of honor
if one stood against all
elements.

Now it's a societal badge of
outcast, laughter, and
ridicule among
peers.

Of saying you're
not good enough
to be with someone.
A pariah among society.

That's why I choose
to walk alone.

I do me. The rest are labels.

10/24/17

"Father"

Piece by piece
is given
and sometimes taken
for granted.

As a father
that's what's expected,
and that's what we do.

In the end,
we give and give
so we're not
the last one
standing in life.

10/26/17

"Boom"

if someone would have told me
that women break your heart
worse when you're older,
I'd still take the chance.

Heartbreak and pain
are old friends of mine.
I'm here to tell you,
even if I could see the future,
I would still take the chance.

Sometimes, you have to
go through pain
to get something good
out of life.

10/26/17

"Closure"

Who'd've thought love would
come at a price?

Who'd've thought that same
price would come with a
consequence?

The closure of hearts is
the price others have
to pay.

10/26/17

"Forward"

We've made our mistakes
to show you we're human.

We've gone without
so you can have.

We come down hard
so you know we truly care.

We love you unconditionally
so you know how to do
your children someday.

We only hope someday
you pass those lessons
on to yours.

10/26/17

"Listen"

Listen to your heart
not your habits.
If you don't know the
what's what,
then you better start
listening.

10/26/17

"Tequila"

Smooth with a
bit of harshness.
Made of gold
but comes correct
with a simple truth.

Not many folks
can handle your
blunt truth
or your taste.

A damn tough
pill to swallow,
but you make the
roughest days
vanish with your presence.

That's the kind
of bitch
you are.

10/28/17

"All of the above"

if you want
his time
his love
his respect
his loyalty

earn it

he's already
trying to do
all of the
above

10/29/17

"Can't Compete"

good men
can't compete
with bad boys
and the women
who want them

that fight
was lost
before
it began

10/30/17

"It's all good"

yeah she loves and needs you
after the other nigga went
and did his thing with his
"side and yeah she rides it"
chick

she's lost lonely confused
but so are you
you've tried to be there
for her and good to her
but you can't compete
not when her side
"tag a bitch an' dip" stick
is there

walk on, son
there's more out there than
what she can offer
be patient, be patient, be patient
good things do come
time to let that heart
heal up and get back to life

she's waiting for you
that good one and yes
there's a good one for you
they still exist among
the shitstorm of bitter women
played by the bad boys they

love oh so much

you got this, son
keep your head up
walk tall and proud
she's waiting for you

10/30/17

"Life"

I'm a moment in time
I'm a dust mote in the universe
I'm here to make something
of my time
I'm here to make the most
of an opportunity
An opportunity called Life

Given a chance
Given a nod
Given the hand I've been dealt
to make the most of this
precious gift...

Life

11/4/17

"You"

For the *fellas,*
be more than what
society or women
or a song tells you
what you are.

Look in the mirror,
listen to the reflection.
Look in your heart,
listen to it talk.

You're not perfect,
you never will be.
Decide to just be
better than you
were yesterday.

Start today...
by accepting
yourself.

11/4/17

"Fuck"

Must be nice to go on
with your life while
others pick up the pieces.

You gotta show me how

the *fuck* you do that,

so I can move the
fuck on!

11/8/17

"Circles"

You one day realize
that a big circle isn't
always a good one.

That a big circle isn't
the best protection,
but another obstacle.

As time passes on,
you see that
the smaller your
circle, the better
protection it provides.

11/8/17

"Never"

Never forget who you are.
Never forget your purpose.
Never forget what makes you strong.

11/10/17

"Trapped"

A trapped heart is one that will break
free by any means.

Trust me, no one can trap a wild animal,
or cage its heart.

Both are deadly, and when freed,
dangerous.

11/09/17

"A demon called Tequila"

You fucked around and did it again, didn't you?
Got in your old pain and your fuck buddy
Tequila visited for a quickie.
Fucked around and left your
head spinning worse than before,
but you love the way she dry-humped
your ass and you're begging for more.

Two nights in a row she visits,
sometimes going porn style on you,
sometimes stroking slo-mo while
laughing through a water-color haze.

Slowly she leaves,
and the pain is still there.
You want her numbing loving caress,
and you took the last sip from her body.
Hot damn you can't handle it!
Your head pounds and your world spins.
Fuck, she's abandoning you,
and it comes rushing back.

The pain, the tears.

Fuck, you need another drink.

11/10/17

Storytime: SCARED

She puts the snub-nosed revolver to her temple: CLICK.

"Your turn." She slides the gun across the table and pours herself a shot of whiskey, downing it in one gulp.

He grabs the gun, never taking his eyes off her. He opens the barrel, spins it, and flicks it close. He pulls the trigger. CLICK.

"Your turn." She takes the gun nervously. The familiar sound of opening, spinning, and closing of the barrel. This time, she grabs the whole bottle and pulls a big swig, slamming in on the table. She sees him smirking, still.

Then she looks at the center of the table.

Where the bullets are.

They forgot to load the bullet. Pussies.

11/25/17

"Twisted"

You'd think after years of heartache, pain, and mulling over why love eludes you, a pattern comes back to haunt you.

Falling for the first fucker you see so you won't be alone. Spitting that "I love you" trap so you can hear it back to make you feel better.

Changing who you are like a chameleon to be who they want you to be while they stay the same.

But this is love, right? Change is what you're supposed to do to make them happy and comfortable while you skip on razors to appease them, correct?

Get your shit together. That's not love. That's cowardice. They got you by the genitals, knowing you'll bend over twice on Sunday to make sure they're happy, they're taken care of.

You lost your way again, and this time, you don't know how to find your way back.

That's love for you.

11/25/17

"Foolish"

She plays you close while settling with someone else. She knows you'll stupidly be there, but better to be there than not at all, right?

Wake up and don't play the Fool's Roll, anymore. Someone's waiting for you out there. So start clearing room today and let the good one come in.

Then the one who played you for a fool, will look foolish in the end.

11/25/17

"Done"

been there, done that twice
two women who claimed to love me
but never good enough to stay
with me

11/25/17

"Worthy"

My brother,
your feelings count, too.
Good and bad men exist
just like good and bad
women.

Too many times we're told to
man up, but how do we do
that when there's no worthy
women to man up for?

Don't let the mistakes of
the many
becomes your judgment

Stay strong, stay real,
and know that someone
will see you're not like
the others. And hopefully,
you'll see she's looking for
someone like you.

11/25/17

"Live"

You live for you.
If you can't live for yourself,
you can't live for anyone else.

11/25/17

Storytime: LET'S TALK

It took two failed marriages, one failed long distance relationship, many other women who kept me at friend's length yet wanted girlfriend benefits while they played the field, to make me realize I was being a dumb fuck.

It took many bad thoughts about hurting myself to hopefully get their love and attention to make me realize I'm worth more than their weakness.

It took me being on the outs with my son for a bit to realize he was the one who loved and needed me, and as a single full-time dad, that's what was important.

Single dads have it bad when it comes to love and women coming in to "save" us, or not giving us the time of day because our kids came before their selfish asses. We just want someone to support, love, and build a family together. Not come in and take over because they think we're doing it wrong.

Maybe that's why I've been alone this whole time. I recognize real, not lip service. Show me that you want to be with me, and not keep me at arm's length. There's nothing worse than caring about someone that doesn't give two shits about you, especially being a single dad whose child sees the disrespect. I've had women be real with me, telling

me they come first, and I respected them for that.
That's why I stayed a single dad after a while.

In the end, that's all that matters: Truth. It hurts,
but you get over it.

-PM
11/25/17

VOLUME

2

"Himself"

And the time came
for him to live
happily ever
after.

You might be asking,
"How the hell
did that
happen?"

Simple.

He believed in himself.

-PM
11/25/17

"Strong"

his pain made him strong.
your doubt toughened him.
the world accepted him.

11/25/17

"Cool"

All he wanted was your love, trust, and acceptance.
Then you found it in another man.
That was cool.
He learned nice guys finish last, and he was out the door.
The world taught him nice guys get the best rewards, and it
did.
Now you see him smile the loving smile at her
that should've been yours,
only you wear the bruises of the bad boy.

11/25/17

"Ready"

To all the nice guys reading this...

I hope you find a woman worthy of your love, your inner beauty, your commitment. I hope the day you find your queen, she sees the king before her.

Most of all, I hope she feels your kindness that's ready for her.

11/25/17

"Thank You"

No matter how much I show you I'd be good for you,
your heart tells you that the asshole is better.

Thank you for showing me my heart's
stronger than your weakness.

11/25/17

"Stop Being"

it's time to "stop being"

stop being...
mad
sad
depressed
confused

it's time to start living your life,
and stop being numb

11/25/17

"Pain"

a weak, painful relationship
is like a good workout.
Pain is weakness
leaving the body.

11/25/17

"Dying"

when you stop living, you start dying.

11/25/17

"Not Strong"

when she tells you
you're just friends,
that means she
wouldn't be strong
enough to be
your lady

11/25/17

"So Are You"

She's strong. So are you.
She's independent. So are you.
She says "me" and "I" too much.
You say "us" and "we" profusely.

Fucking tell me how far
your relationship will last...

11/25/17

"Be You"

Be who you are, but don't knock the other person for being them.

11/25/17

"Gone"

The fuck you crying for again!
Don't let them see your tears.
Save them when they're really need!

The fuck you crying for now?
Be tough and stand strong.
Don't let their words weaken you!

The fuck you hanging your head for?
Pick your damn head up, patna.
Stand tall, don't diminish your power!

Now, doesn't that feel better?
Tougher, stronger, more powerful
because your fucks are gone!

11/25/17

"Yourself"

Know yourself. Be yourself. Love yourself.

11/25/17

"How They Love You"

you know when you've found a good person
when they don't take your pain away,
but show you how it makes you grow,
and to give you the love
that was waiting for you.

11/25/17

"Self Love"

Love yourself before relying on someone else's.

11/25/17

"Shame"

It's a damn shame when you can sit
next to the "one you love" and still
be just as lonely before you
two met

11/25/17

"Ugly"

Fuck no pretty packages don't mean pretty insides.
Some of the ugliest people I've met have been the prettiest
ones.
When you lack substance, you lack soul.

11/25/17

"Bouncer"

It's a blessing and curse,
that the one job I loved and hated,
has kept me going in life.
Kept me going when all else has failed.

The life of a bouncer.

Can't stop, won't stop.

11/25/17

"Jam"

Jam to your own groove.
No one can take that from you.

11/25/17

"All"

don't waste your time on those
not willing to give you their all

-PM
11/25/17

"Gametime"

Love is a game, remember?
Hope you like the consequences.

-PM
11/25/17

"Dwell"

Dwelling in the past means you dwell on mistakes. Take those past mistakes and turn them into triumphs by forging a life for yourself. Prove to yourself you're worth a damn, and fuck what the past whispers in your ear.

-PM

11/25/17

"Real"

Let's be real.
How many in your life
will walk with you through
the good and bad times?
How many will protect, love,
and honor you like you do them?

Fuck that noise about time and distance.
Life isn't a meme.
Protect those who protect you.
Those that choose to drop off
weren't strong enough to stand
by your side from jump.

-PM

11/25/17

"Wounds"

Time doesn't heal all wounds.
Some are meant to stay open
as a reminder of what could happen again.

-PM

11/25/17

"The Way"

Make an impact in someone's life.
Show others that all isn't lost.
Help someone to be strong the way
you showed yourself how to stand alone.
Teach someone that all fights
aren't won with fists,
but with your heart and instinct.

That way, when the time comes
for them to show someone to be strong,
they'll know the way.

-PM

11/25/17

"Live this Life"

To whoever reads this...

Know your strength, your courage, your love, your anger.
Teach yourself to stand when all else seems lost,
teach yourself to get back up when knocked down.

Help yourself understand the difference
between a helping hand
and a closed fist.
Help others who need it
but teach others to help themselves.

Fall in love, be love.
Jump in with both feet and risk openness.
Know if you do have to walk away,
you know you gave it your all.

Accept the seasons.
Each carries its sweet and sour
and is meant to test you.
Face those tests head on,
come out better than you were
whether you passed or failed.

In the end, this is called Life.
Live it, so it doesn't live you.

-PM
11/25/17

VOLUME

3

Storytime: THERE CAN BE ONLY ONE

Be You, Do you.

We hear that shit often, but hard to do. Why? We're still too busy trying to be accepted by others. Fuck that noise when you say you don't. That's bullshit. We all do. I've done it.

I found a way to somewhat beat it.

Come closer, and I'll tell you.

Live your life. That's it, that simple. Live your life.

Live it with passion, live it with purpose. Take a look at your life and see if it's what you want, but you have to honest with yourself.

Is it working for you? Are you making moves that make that life you wanted possible?

Maybe you're pointing the finger at everyone for not being where you are in life. Take a look at your actions then at your "jailers". Deep down, you know it's you. Stand up for yourself and tell them to fuck off. Then look in the mirror and tell yourself the same thing because you allowed it.

Tell the voices, all the doubters, all the things that you feel are keeping you back to fuck off. Don't let others weakness become yours. I'm telling you from experience, that once you let the voices of doubt get in your head, they never leave. They try to beat you at every turn. Just when you feel things are going good and you're about to make positive changes in your life, they pop back up like that life-long pimple that sticks around well into adulthood (yes, adults still get pimples and shit).

Push past all that pain, because that's what it is. Wait, fuck that...EMBRACE IT! People don't embrace shit, they'd rather circumvent it. As we say in the bar life, embrace the chaos. Feel that radical energy? It's there for a reason! Don't fight it, use it. Absorb that shit, let it strengthen you. Vibe with it, use it.

You have one shot. Make it count.

-PM
12/23/17

"Love Me"

love me like no other man matters,
not when it's convenient for you.

p.m.
12.23.2017

Remembering

I remember your last words to me,
"Know you're loved."

In one night, you taught me to be myself,
taught me that mistakes happen
and that the past doesn't define me.
Only what happens now.

You looked inside me,
knew me like you did all these years,
and broken as I was,
you were ready to give a man
struggling as a single dad a
chance at knowing what it was like
to be loved for both our sakes.

You were taken, but I didn't forget
how you loved me.
Won't forget those oh-so deep
kisses that touched my soul.
MMM, I knew what Heaven was
again, and I thank you for
showing me that.

12.23.17

Walk In Beauty

My son's moved on,
trying his best to find
his place in this crazy world.
Walk in Beauty, mijo.
It's a crazy beautiful place out there.

12.24.17

Labels

Saint, sinner, bouncer, Taurus, lover,
boyfriend, bother, son, homie, friend,
enemy, a waste, dramatic, competent,
lazy, fucker, half-breed, nigger, spic,
unpatriotic, bodyguard, enforcer,
drug dealer, banger, traitor, nerd,
geek, terrorist.

So many labels I'm known by except for
one: ME.

12.24.17

"You Got This"

2018 is coming.
This is your time to shine,
to expand on what's Within.
You got this.
Get out your own way,
Embrace the Motherfuckin' Chaos
like a long-lost lover.
You got this.
It's your time to shine, baby!
No more excuses,
no more bullshit.
You got this.
I believe in you.

-PM

Smoke

The **fuck** is wrong with you?
The physical is a distraction.
Get beneath the surface
so you won't get twisted again
and blame your bad
on someone else.

12.30.17

Tango

People want and need
Love in their lives, yet become professional
tango dancers when it
comes to Love.
Someday we'll get it, that
we've all been hurt,
and doing the Tango
should be
done on the dance floor,
and not in our hearts.

1.3.18

Step Off

There's a problem when people
in your life don't love and respect
you the way you do them. That's
called disrespect. Clear them
out of your life, don't allow them
to continue to occupy space
when someone else can fill the
gap with good soul food. You
deserve better, but only if you
take the step to do better.

1.3.18

Quantify

It's not about the quantity of
people who come into your life,
but the quality of people who
hang until the end.

1.12.18

Just Right

Too Black for the Mexicans,
too Mexican for the Blacks,
the one thing that matters most,
I'm just right for me.

1.16.18

Parting words for 2017...

Embrace the changes of yesterday, so they
can make you a better person in the present.

Don't worry about the future, it's not the
gift that's meant for you to enjoy right now.
That's why we live in the present.

--PM

Vibe

Babygirl,
Respect is earned, not given.
I know you've been through some
shit, but so have I.
I don't have it all figured
out, but our struggle together
might be the medicine
we're both looking for.

No, you don't owe me a
damn thing. I have to
earn everything with you.
Love, truth, faith, honor.
Guess what? You being a
broken woman doesn't
make you exempt.
I've been hurt just like
you.

Together, we can vibe and
beat these demons
back with an ugly stick, or
at best, own them.
Together, we can work
magic, the kind that's
just for us.

I'm willing to do work,
whatever it takes to vibe
with your life.

Are you?

Situation

Honor your
feelings of pain
and frustration.

It means you
care about

the situation.

1.23.18

Untitled

Live your life like
no one else matters.
Wake up every day
with the purpose
of only doing for you.

Then, years from
now, when you've done
all that, tell me
how alone you are.

Staying in your lane
is good, but is
it always worth
walking alone?

1.24.18

Never Do

We can never do right
when everyone thinks
we're doing wrong.

When we prove we're
not like the others,
we still don't catch a
break.

Men who do what's
right, not what's
easiest. Men who
want families but
get taken advantage
of. Our pride is
attacked, our dignity,
all because of the
bad actions of another.

We live in a world
where we get emasculated,
humiliated, all because the
actions of a few that
mess it up for us.

1.24.18

Whirlwind Tour

I want to jump out of a plane at 15,000 feet and open
the chute at 2000 feet on my birthday.

I want to bake a birthday cake so damn big
it could feed 10,000 people and everyone
would think it's the best goddamn cake ever!

I want to swim out in the middle of the
ocean and attempt to stupidly look down
to the bottom, where the last remnants
of beauty are, before my fellow humans
allow corporations to taint that as well.

I want to make homes for the needy here
in the United States, instead of going across
the world building homes. I'd be nice to
do for folks here as well who need it.

Most of all, I want my family to prosper,
my son to be joyous and give me grandkids,
and to be remembered not as an author,
but as a genuine human being.

I want to be remembered as...ME!

1.25.18

Storytime: THANK YOU

Hell yeah I've grown a little jaded and cynical
over the years. I let Life do me, instead of the
opposite.

That's not a bad thing.

Life taught me to toughen up, not everything
will go my way, not everyone will accept me,
be grateful for what I have because there are
those that don't have shit, and to hold tight to
those who Walk The Line with me.

It's our struggles and experiences that make us
who we are, but we have a choice every day
on who and how we want to spend our lives.

I thank Life every day for me being here, despite
what's happened. Fuck yeah, I'm a little jaded
and cynical, but I'm built for this life, this
crazy adventure of heartbreak, joys, failures,
loves, tequila, sex, single fatherhood, misfits,
radio DJ'ing, bouncing, video gaming...

This Life that's be thrown at me, that's my challenge,
my strength, my weakness, and best of all,
Life really did let me choose the road less traveled.

1.26.18

"Waste"

Don't waste your time
on those not willing
to give you their all.

1.26.18

"Please Read"

If you're reading this...

Know that you are always stronger than a hater's weakness.

1.27.18

Watch and Learn

All it takes is for you to sit back and watch people show their true colors and show where you stand with them.

-pm

"Hello 2018"

I hope you learned many lessons in 2017.
That way, 2018 will be the year you apply
them for your betterment.

-Phillip Magana

"Not Strong"

When she tells you you're just friends,
that means she won't be strong enough to be
your lady.

-Phillip Magana

"Groove"

Jam to your own groove.
No one can take that from you.

Why The Fuck

Why the fuck don't people smile more?
Why the fuck don't people laugh more?
Why the fuck don't people love more?
Why the fuck don't people live more?

Smile, Laugh, Love, Live. You got one
shot. Stop giving a fuck what noise you
here, and do you.

-PM

"Magic"

When you find your soul, you
find your music. That's when the
magic happens.

-PM

MID CREDITS (JUST LIKE THE MCU MOVIES)

Well, if you got this far, it means you liked the book, or you finished it "just because". Either way, thank you for sharing this particular journey with me. It was hella fun getting this book together as well as writing it. Making the book was as much a journey as my other ones, and this was a big fucking learning experience!

A shoutout to a few folks who helped read the material, or gave emotional support:

My Son, Anthony
My Mom
Certain friends and family
My dawgs Lorel and Laurel
Deana
Soul Friend Shelly
My W, Becki
All my peeps I consider bros and sis
The people who doubted me
The folks who believed in me

This is for you!

I shall be telling this with a sigh
Somewhere ages and ages hence:
Two roads diverged in a wood, and I—
I took the one less traveled by,
And that has made all the difference.

-Robert Frost

About the Author

Born and raised on Earth,
made Flagstaff, AZ his soul spot.

Father to Anthony, son to Carmen and Sanders.

Hated by many, truly loved by few.

Made mistakes, made better decisions.

A fighter, a dad, a loner, ice cream lover,
BBQ fanatic, adventurer to the soul. Maybe
someday, I'll see you on a trail somewhere.
Let's build a fire, make some S'mores,
down some tequila, tell some stories!

Thanks for reading. Peace!